Once Out of Nature

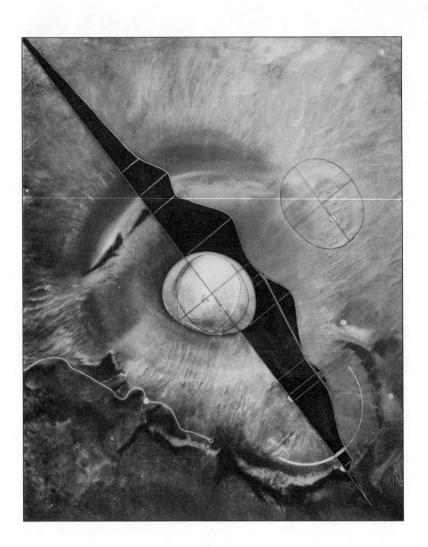

Jim Simmerman

Once Out of Nature

THE GALILEO PRESS LTD

Copyright © 1989 by Jim Simmerman

Published by The Galileo Press, Ltd., 15201 Wheeler Lane, Sparks, MD 21152

Production by Kachergis Book Design, Pittsboro, NC

Cover art: aerial photo of Roden Crater, by James Turrell. Reprinted with permission of James Turrell.

Publication of this book was made possible in part by a grant from the Maryland State Arts Council.

Library of Congress Cataloging-in-Publication Data

Simmerman, Jim, 1952–
 Once out of nature : poems / by Jim Simmerman. — 1st ed.
  p. cm.
 ISBN 0-913123-20-X : $15.95 (est.)
 ISBN 0-913123-21-8 : $9.95 (est.)
 I. Title.
PS3569.I472605 1988   88-18062
811'.54—dc19   CIP

FIRST EDITION

Acknowledgments

I would like to thank the editors of the following publications, in which many of these poems, or versions thereof, have appeared.

Black Star: "Boys"

Bloomsbury Review: "Five Love Poems to No One"

Cimarron Review: "Against Derrida" (and the *Glosse* of "Against Derrida" by Jay Farness) reprinted here with the permission of the Board of Regents of Oklahoma State University, holders of the copyright

Crazyhorse: "Sure the Oak" and "Then Again"

Kansas Quarterly: "Child's Grave, Hale County, Alabama"

Laurel Review: "December," "Philly's Garden," and "The Swallows, Their Song"

New England Review and Bread Loaf Quarterly: "Hide-and-go-seek," "The Last Word" (under the title "Division of Property"), "Once Out of Nature," and "With Shadows"

Northern Arizona Review: "Even the Silence" and "The Rumor"

Poetry: "Almost Dancing," "Fetch," "FINALLY," "The Gulls," and "Lighthouse"

Poetry Miscellany: "A Teapot" and "Where the Echo Waits"

Quarry West: "Wood for the Winter"

Quarterly West: "Roden Crater"

Shankpainter: "Skin Flick" and "Zombies"

Sonora Review: "A Rainbow"

Western Humanities Review: "Open Season"

"Almost Dancing" was reprinted in *The Music of What Happens: Poems That Tell Stories* (Orchard Books, 1988).

"Child's Grave, Hale County, Alabama" and "Hide-and-go-seek" were reprinted in *Bread Loaf Anthology of Contemporary American Poetry* (University Press of New England, 1985), where "Whatever It Is" was first published.

"Child's Grave, Hale County, Alabama" was also reprinted in *Pushcart Prize X: Best of the Small Presses* (Pushcart Press, 1985).

"Roden Crater" was reprinted in *Occluded Front*, a book on the work of artist James Turrell (copublished by Lapis Press, the Fellows of Contemporary Art, and the Museum of Contemporary Art in Los Angeles, 1985).

"Then Again" was reprinted in *Anthology of Magazine Verse & Yearbook of American Poetry* (Monitor Book Company, 1985) and in *Crossing the River: Poets of the Western United States* (Permanent Press, 1987).

"Zombies" was reprinted in *Anthology of Magazine Verse & Yearbook of American Poetry* (Monitor Book Company, 1988).

Several of the poems herein were collected as a chapbook, *Bad Weather*, published by Ocotillo Press in 1988.

I would also like to thank the Arizona Commission on the Arts, the Fine Arts Work Center (Provincetown, Massachusetts), the National Endowment for the Arts, and Northern Arizona University for fellowships and grants which afforded me time to work on this book.

for the Moans,
for Lo

"Once out of nature I shall never take
My bodily form from any natural thing . . . "

"Sailing to Byzantium"
W.B. YEATS

Contents

1

Where the Echo Waits 3
Once Out of Nature 4
A Teapot 6
Child's Grave, Hale County, Alabama 7
Fetch 9
Lighthouse 10

2

The Last Word 13
Five Love Poems to No One 14
A Rainbow 15
The Swallows, Their Song 17
December 19
Even the Silence 21

3

The Rumor 25
Open Season 26
Boys 27
Skin Flick 28
Against Derrida 30
FINALLY 35

4

Hide-and-go-seek 39
With Shadows 40
Zombies 42
Wood for the Winter 44
Philly's Garden 46
Whatever It Is 48

5

Sure the Oak   51

Then Again   53

Almost Dancing   55

The Gulls   58

Roden Crater   59

A Lick and a Prayer   62

Notes   65

1

Where the Echo Waits

Something died before I could get this written.
Now it won't have to apologize for anything anymore.
Now it can live like a windchime in a vacuum,
With a shovel's tenacity and the dignity of a hole.

Now, if I listen to the clock's iron lung,
I can hear it breathing in the lull between ticks.
If I look into the driest wash of an arroyo,
I can see it floating face down in the rocks.

At night the threads of its coat unravel
And lash the sleeping watchman to his dream.
Closed books expunge themselves
To begin anew as roots, as buried things.

Blown-out treads along the sides of interstates
Flap themselves into great dark birds, soar.
Lost coins drift to the river's roof.
Stone madonnas turn to face the chapel door.

Something died, and without witness.
It falls through the night like rain through rain.
Look for it in the shadow cast by a shadow. Wait for it
Where the echo waits for someone to call its name.

Once Out of Nature

The pines go up and down like spines without brains.
They don't pay attention and they don't take notes.
They hang out in gangs like the hard guys from high school
Who spit for a living and likely got fucked.

I go up and down the side of the mountain
With my feet futzing forward like whiz kids on dope.
I tromple through weeds that don't know they're not flowers
In the foyer of heaven, where nobody smokes.

Sometimes it rains and my sneakers smooch mud.
Sometimes a whirligig hitches a ride.
A sign says *No Trespassing This Means You*—
Dufus, shit-for-brains—this means your life.

This means that snot-freezing day on Cape Cod
Dozens of gulls flopped dead down from the sky
Like they had just flunked flying or been expelled
From the species and I had to decide

Whether to pick my way among them
Or pick them up by their wing tips and pitch them
Like so many lame excuses for gulls
Out into the Atlantic's contemptuous phlegm.

I know they were only idiot beasts,
Slightly retarded like Dennis Harper
Who tooled crude birds and billy-clubs in shop
And once, when he found out I was still a virgin,

Offered me his girlfriend for the night.
I could decide to think of him here,
Where a creek wisenheimers its way through the woods
And a scoff-bird twitters *so what? who cares?*

Where a single, inexplicable red
High-heeled shoe molders by a fallen pine,

Where the same dumb heart keeps reciting the same
Dumb spondee—*duh, duh*—trying to make it sing.

I could decide to think of the night
Eighteen years back Harper let his body glide
On the wings of a drug so pure he almost crooned
Let me out of the car. I think I'm going to die.

Some things you can't take back though—
You take them with you the rest of your life,
Kicking them over like a shoe or a bird,
Like eventually they might dance, might fly;

Like when the squawking stops, the silence starts singing
With nothing to hear it or hear if it ends. . . .
Let me out of the car. I had to decide.
I think I'm going to die. And we did.

A Teapot

Worn red like weathered adobe.
Gilded at the crown like stained-glass saints.
My grandmother gave it to me
The year before she died,
The year before I left my three
Plastic cups, my two chipped plates,
My one-room shoebox of a loft
To hitchhike the rain-steeped Pacific Northwest,
Looking for anything distant or golden,
Without a phone number or an address.
There are three gaudy flowers
Sketched on its side.
They recall corsages
Impuissant old ladies wear to church,
Or the extravagant bouquet
Left, once a year, in a cemetery—
As if all that sweet decay
Could take root in the faltered heart,
Which asks of us nothing
But to be hid away.
The glued-on handle is curled like an ear
That seems to be listening
For a phone to ring,
For the voice of a grandson lost somewhere
In the gray blur of a coastal town—
Cars humming slowly home,
Their headlamps on,
Their wipers tocking like metronomes:
The inclement music
Of something gone wrong.
And looking inside, I see it is stained
With the cumulus sludge
Of all that has brewed;
All that the leaves,
Could I have read them, foretold:
Rain pouring prodigally then,
Then today, like nothing I could hold.

Child's Grave, Hale County, Alabama

Someone drove a two-by-four
through the heart of this hard land
that even in a good year
will notch a plow blade worthless,
snap the head off a shovel,
or bow a stubborn back.
He'd have had to steal
the wood from a local mill
or steal, by starlight, across
his landlord's farm, to worry
a fencepost out of its well
and lug it the three miles home.
He'd have had to leave his wife
asleep on a cornshuck mat,
leave his broken brogans
by the stove, to slip outside,
lullaby soft, with the child
bundled in a burlap sack.
What a thing to have to do
on a cold night in December,
1936, alone
but for a raspy wind
and the red, rock-ridden dirt
things come down to in the end.
Whoever it was pounded
this shabby half-cross
into the ground must have toiled
all night to root it so:
five feet buried with the child
for the foot of it that shows.
And as there are no words
carved here, it's likely that
the man was illiterate,
or addled with fatigue,
or wrenched simple-minded
by the one simple fact.
Or else the unscored lumber

driven deep into the land
and the hump of busted rock
spoke too plainly of his grief—
forty years laid by and still
there are no words for this.

Fetch

The marrow of it's this:
that night after night I dream
you alive, dream you clawing
up and through the snarl
of spade-lopped roots and loam,
through the cairn beneath the pine
in a bower of pines, a wildwood
of pines, beneath a wheeling moon—
shaking from your body
the tattered blanket, shaking
from your throat the collar
of blood—the ball
in your mouth where I left it,
your coat wet where I kissed it—
breaking through underbrush
onto the trail, tracking it back
to the tire-rutted road—
loping now, running now—
your nostrils flared
and full of the world—
ignoring the squirrel,
ignoring the jay, ignoring
the freeway's litter of bones—
night nearly dead as you
bolt for the lane,
up the drive, into the yard—
panting now, breathing now—
racing from door to window to door,
scratching at the screen,
whining at the glass, the ball
in your mouth—Lo,
wouldn't I shake from this
sweet gnawed dream to rise
and fetch you in,
with the light that returns
me day after day,
takes you again and again.

Lighthouse

Nothing, and no one, and never again . . .
I want to say it's not like that—the world
I mean, that darkling sea where nothing stays
On course for long, where winds go mad, where things
Go down and don't come back.

                              They don't come back
And don't come back and still you stand your
Lonesome watch—a granite wall too sheer to scale,
An iron door that won't unlock. I want
To say it matters, but the swells blow up
And drown my voice.

                         A lighthouse rises north
Of here; its beacon sweeps the night. I want
To say there's comfort there for every vessel
Off its way or stranded on some buried
Shoal; for every lost, unlooked for sail—
I want to see them home.

                            Never again,
And again, and again . . . The tide returns
Alone. I want to say it's dignity
Has made us so alike by now I'm almost
You, my fogged-up eyes awake for anything
Afloat out there, anything to save.

2

The Last Word

You can have the bright
face of the full moon
if I can have the dark
one it keeps out of sight.

You can have the circles
we chased ourselves in
if I can have the empty
tunnels inside.

You can have the past
and the future to boot
if I can have the nick
of time in between.

You can have the warmth
from the bridges we burned
if I can have the ashes
drifting downstream.

You can have the music
that marshaled the waltz
if I can have the echo
that died in the rafters.

You can have the last
word, whatever it is,
if I can have all
the silence thereafter.

Five Love Poems to No One

There was a knock and then there wasn't.
There was a door and then there wasn't.
There was a knock, a door. . . .

*

I follow your footprints across the wet grass.
They lead to a river black as anthracite
And a boat without oars.

*

Sleep is a desert that lets me return.
The saguaros raise their arms as in welcome.
Their roots stay buried, safe from touch.

*

There is a letter crumpled in the garden.
If it were an orchid, it would wither.
If a bird, fly away.

*

Goodbye I say to the wing in the woods.
Goodbye to the squandered word.
Yesterday, yesterday: hole inside a hole. . . .

A Rainbow

If we'd known where to begin
we wouldn't've wound up where we did—
smack-dab lost in Somewhere, Massachusetts,
with a river for a guardrail
and a rainstorm for a road map.
We were two sleepy puppies
on the hearsay of a scent.
We were one sorry carload of hung-over baggage
bucking a two-lane slick as silk pajamas
and yammering like grocers
just to stay awake.
But the obvious is only obvious
when it's obvious: we had to brake
into a Burger King to find out where we were—
"What did they ask you?" someone asked
the kid we'd had to ask; and when he answered:
"What did you tell 'em?" Indeed,
we'd as well've been anywhere then—
a couple bald Rapunzels
and half in love at that.
It was Sunday was all we knew, and raining.
We were lost and low on gas.
Like a poem that didn't know where it was going
we talked fast and drove—
two in a car and one thing clear,
then luminous: a rainbow. . . .
The better part of an hour that bantam
dreamstuff of a frown
hung half-a-hair offside the road
like something crayoned by a child
who wouldn't stay inside the lines.
Its whole shameless *je ne sais quoi*
was everywhere we weren't—
we were just another vehicle
driving at a tenor.
It was a comic book in church.
But we'd've had to've been a lot smarter
than we were to know how dumb

what we tried to do was—
you can't thread a rainbow's the first
thing we learned; then this:
you can't outrun one. . . .

Ditto the drizzle of *since then*'s since—
months—and the *nothing but miles* between us.
It's like we'd been hitched
to inertia and told,
it's not your responsibility;
it's like we'd been ordered to opposite ends
of a petered-out rainbow,
and told to pay attention
and report back. . . .

If we'd known where to begin
we might've known when to quit,
might've driven headlong into that.

The Swallows, Their Song

If some day you wake and I'm not there—
some ordinary day, some morning
when the sun is low, the wind low, the weather
so mild as to be, almost, an absence—
if you wake to find me gone away
remember how I loved you long, and last.

Nothing stays forever. Nothing lasts.
Remember how swallows nested there,
in the eaves, all summer and the way
their singing woke us early mornings?
How many months we've overslept their absence.
How many things have vanished into weather.

It's days like this I can't determine whether
we've worked a kind of nesting place at last,
or whether what we've worked is just an absence,
a little bed of sticks and no one there.
It's winter now, and dark this time of morning
as if the sun had burned itself away.

It's days like this I see that there are ways
to change and vanish subtly as weather,
as dusk becoming night becoming morning
until there is no saying *long*, or *last*,
but only saying *there, it was there*
until the words have echoed into absence.

It must be I miss the swallows. Their absence
stays, like the nest, until each day is weighed
against it. It must be I miss their
singing, the way it scored such weather
as made love easy so long as it would last.
I did not think it was a song of mourning.

Strange that I should think so now. This morning
the swallows, their song, these six months absent,
seem more real than the empty nest; than last

night when, asleep, you lay so far away
from me, as if lost in some frightful weather,
I saw how far it is from here to there.

Some morning if you wake and I'm not there,
gone away like the swallows, an absence,
remember what weather takes the nest at last.

December

Whether there will be one sweet bird
to stay and sing us through the winter
is not my job to say or guess.
The windfalls in our neighbor's yard—
the heavy fruit we hungered for
a month ago, when life was charm
and all the sky a burnished blue—
are coals beneath our feet.
What leaves remain have turned, have blown
to drifts along the fence.
The year has turned its pockets out:
December. Still you have not left.
Last night I took myself away
to walk the town alone,
picking my way down empty lanes
whose names I did not know.
What piddling light the moon allowed
made stickmen of the trees.
Hours lapsed. As did the wind
which lives nowhere and regrets nothing.
Didn't I crave one battered wing
to gather me and lift me from
that fickle animal, the heart,
and all it had tried to hoard?
Instead, I clambered three flights up
the fire escape of a gutted church
where no one came to pray anymore
or light a candle for the dead,
where silence was the only hymn
and God could finally get some sleep.
I don't say it was heaven there,
but where we lived looked dark and small:
a toy village built by a child
from cardboard boxes, foil, and paste.
The first gray filaments of dawn
had just begun unraveling
across the houses and closed shops,
the vacant lots and salt-gnawed streets.

I knew that you were down there too,
impossibly apart, enclosed
within your own gray thoughts.
I do not think they turned to me.
Then I saw some bird had worked
a nest amid the charred rubble
of that place. And suddenly
the air swelled with a few clear notes,
a shameless flight of song so full
the emptiness went out of me.
I might have stayed a long time there,
but human song needs words:
a bird gave me the melody,
the lyrics came from somewhere else—
from somewhere I could never fly,
could never stumble on alone.
They sang me down the way I came,
sang *Go home, boy. Grow up. Go home.*

Even the Silence

Till they pluck the glass rose
from the cistern of my fist
and replace my name
with two stony lies . . .

Till they siphon
from my ears the music
I couldn't learn to play,
and turn my pockets out

and drop the coins
with their faces and dates
into the wishing wells
of my eyes . . .

Till they cross my arms so,
set my lips so—
the words I never spoke well
stunted there forever . . .

Till they take back the world—
take it back
like something never meant—
the world that bore me up

and on whose shoulders
I tried to ride lightly;
and all I tended
as best I knew how;

and the stoplight
pulsing off a wet, black street
you might walk alone then,
awhile . . .

Love, could you love me
according to my nature,

I would love you for nothing
but the weather of your heart,

where words could be clouds
they're so flimsy, so fleeting,
then—even the silence
bespeaking my troth.

3

The Rumor

Alone I'm a secret I keep from myself
the way a dream doesn't know it's a dream
in which six black ducks drift out from the shore
not knowing they're ducks, or the sea a sea,

not knowing how deep the water beneath them,
how empty the sky above. . . . On the odd
chance you hear of me, don't tell a soul.
A soul is a gossip. I'm rumor enough.

Open Season

I'm tired of spring
the trees flaunting
their green the birds
sneaking back like a
flock of nasty rumors
monotonous as sheets
the April sky what
say we invent a new
season three times
pungent as crime what
say we fill it with
exotic diseases and
give it a name no one
can pronounce let's
extinguish the tribes
of shrubbery deport
the proletarian egg
like any competent
vandal or someone
just a little sick
of daffodils let's
conjure up some real
pestilence if anything
be cute or even
furry let's beat it
with a rake I mean
it's only fair it's
only human to want a
change what say we
invent a real punch
line to evolution
what say open
season on anything
skulking into May.

Boys

Peggy thought she was a brontosaurus.
We didn't tell her different.
We thought we were in the fifth grade
in Arkansas, in 1963,
and if you lost your marbles,
finders keepers.
We'd seen dogs
and thought we knew where to stick it.

When Peggy pulled her hair out
and stuck band-aids to her head,
the teacher made her wear mittens.
When you finished an apple
and said, "Apple core,"
someone chimed "Baltimore,"
then you said, "Who's your friend?"
and he said, and you threw it. . . .

Peggy roared,
but we knew what was fair.
If you disturbed the class
you had to stand in the trash.
If you touched
a retard you had to wash your hands quick.
If girls were smart as boys,
why did they wear dresses?

When we started sixth grade,
Peggy didn't.
We hardly missed her.
We thought she was extinct.
When the girls jumped rope,
We saw England and France.
We were boys being boys.
We hit hard. We ran fast.

Skin Flick

The kid with the rhinestone cockring
is prolific alright.
He can diddle the blonde, the twin
brunettes, the midget and the collie
three times apiece,
and that's not counting retakes.
Me, I'm another stealthy
patron of the arts
with an aisle to myself
and my hat in my lap;
I'm a tourist on the wrong bus
to everywhere in particular,
and the signs flashing past read
Hell in a Handbasket.
Hey, I know the girls on screen
most likely have kin
in Sioux Falls or Duluth.
Who knows but one
loved English once:
the classroom darling
reciting Hopkins and Frost.
What she does with her
lips just now, Modest Reader,
I don't need to tell—
undoubtedly you know the one
about the girl from Savannah,
the parrot, the banana. . . .
It's an old joke, and bad,
but even I admit
a limerick's a poem.
And what those children
of accountants and grocers
are doing up there
in myriad mathematical machinations—
close-ups, fade-outs;
the microphone hidden lord-knows-where—
is also acting,
and some of it good!

I'm willing to grant
the director his vision.
Even the dog had to learn its part.
And the kid with the cockring
can come on cue,
like a good line of Yeats
or Williams will do.

Coda: Masturbation

Don't think of poetry.

Against Derrida

Terrific, another post-
structural exegesis of death
as signant or text

as kaleidoscope. Meanwhile,
I'm a romantic with a whale's
eye view of Ahab. That is,

I mean to make more of things
than things mean to make of me.
Twice at least I've been privy

to the sort of silence Melville
sank to and the sea,
that cradle of claws and bottled

mail, said mum's the word
and all the soggy sails agreed.
If the world's a rondeau

as your realist would have
us chant, there's no direction
safe to spit in,

nor lacuna, nor end-stop,
though an occasional gull
on the horizon scans. I don't

know much about the whale
as utterance, the coin
nailed to the mast as trope.

But when the ship goes down
with its cargo of catharsis,
some fool will forge a fresh

and voluminous conceit:
flotsam on the empty page, words
like headstones lost at sea.

GLOSSE

l.1   *post-*: gloss to ll.12–13, "bottled mail," addresses this; *Derrida/Terrific*: if not Romantic irony, sarcasm then.

ll.2–3   *death/as signant*: paranomasia of cygnet or cygnant (presumably "swanlike"), alluding to the symbolism of Yeats, for one, where the swan's immortality mocks the writer's mortality, here foreshadowing "headstones lost at sea" (l.30); thus with such a cygnant the poem would take off, at first as a sort of "winged white whale," if the glosser might venture to say so.

l.6   *Ahab*: the Derridean alter-ego inscribed with alphabetic laughter ("alphabet" from the Greek a-b); here a-b, a synecdoche for the grapheme, is ruptured by "Ha!"—*viz.*, the general play of Nietzsche's gay science (for gaiety, see below) as spelled out by the derisive Derrida.

ll.6,7   *eye/I*: the poet gathers speed for flight in a venerable pun of the Romanticist voy(ag)eur; also a reference to nautical jargon—"Aye, aye!"—and to the disingenuously Ishmael-like pretense of the poem—"Yes, yes!"—against the Ahabian Derrida.

ll.10–11   *silence Melville/sank to*: an appeal to authority, derivation, and literary property; also a clever self-contradiction inasmuch as a silence bruited by Melville is no longer strictly speaking a silent silence; with this silent sinking the poet's song has, by the way, finally risen in full flight.

ll.12–13   *bottled/mail*: a remarkable dissemy of the seaworthy poet, alluding to the general problem of "post" (l.1) or *envoi* in Derrida, but also—as bottled *male*—to the storing of the boiled *sperm* whale in *Moby-Dick*, and thus also to the question of Queequeg and Ishmael and of Melville's alleged homosexuality, and therefore to related unspecified practices of lusty men at sea which, as Wittgenstein might say, we must consign to silence; all this now teems with dissemination.

l.13   *mum's the word*: conspicuously *not* the Johannine doctrine of the *logos*; *mum* and its letters here also palindromes and paradigms of the poem's reversible travels; also a tangle here of deceptively learned, far-reaching references, first to the tradition of pantomime (*mumming*) as a model of the text (see Derrida on Mallarmé's *Mimique*), but also to Greek *muō*, "to close one's eyes" (cf. ll.5–6 and the pretense of the seer), and also to Greek *mueō*, "to initiate into the mysteries," as of those of the Mother ("Mum") at Eleusis. The hypotyposis of the family scene in the poet's personal symbolism is well known.

ll.15–17   *If the world's a,* etc.: the poet echoes Stevens's manner in words ironically attributed to a "realist." The poet's missives hereafter allude to various filler items of the Derridean old world news. For example, note that the midpoint of the poem's journey by word count (a word count undertaken to ensure that the gloss exceeds the text) falls between "'s" and "a," this being a hermetic reference to SA (a mystic logo in Derrida and others as well as a loose frenchification of "Mum's" [l.13]).

l.18   *spit*: some might mistakenly direct this telling rattle in the throat toward Fr. *Glas* (*not* pronounced "gloss"), but what the poet means to say is that, unlike a child fathoming the abyss with expectorant, not even the spit of a poet can fall through the webs of textuality to "reality" without getting caught up in signification and contextualizing as here, as now.

l.19   *end-stop*: another deconstructive blazon has "stop" undoing the sense of "end" (if "end" really were, why supplement it with "stop"?) and, naturally, importing the question of *différance*.

ll.21–22   *I don't know/much about*: another intertext, perhaps even suggested background music for the reading, this a hook from Sam Cooke's anti-intellectual, reggae-esque "What a Wonderful World," and so behind the poet's *fausse* naïveté sounds an allusion (1) to Melville's South Seas heterocosmos and to *tristes tropiques* and (2) to Ishmael's subjunctive affirmation ("what a wonderful world it would be").

l.23   *coin*: i.e., koine, a lingua franca, here likening different language theories to views of Ahab's doubloon; the poet himself in a giddy moment has suggested that *coin* might be an anagram of *icon* ("I con"? the scanned gull, ll.20–21?), which shows, the glosser might add, how much poets know of these matters.

l.24   *trope*: clearly *rope* attached to a mast or *t*; in this way suggesting the page itself becoming like a mast with sail needing the rigging of the poet's lines.

l.25   *But when the ship goes down*: i.e., the ship fitted out in the previous gloss, here so speedy and tragic a loss, but then so deep a climax for so short a poem! For the *topos* of poem as ship, see Dante, Spenser, *et al.*

l.26   *cargo of catharsis*: the storied "purge downwards," apparently a reference to the tragic sinking of this poem into silence, perhaps from semiotic overload. The scandalous sense of *Pequod*'s "cargo of catharsis," remember, we have also consigned to such silence in the gloss to ll.12–13, though were he to speak here, the glosser might say how the poem, despite its dismembered appearance, is at once black ship, white whale, and read everywhere.

ll.26–27   *c, c, f, f, f*: the alliteration of these lines heralds the apotheosis of *flotsam*—cf. sea litter, sea *litterae*, deconstructed words from overseas at a loss without a gloss.

l.28   *voluminous conceit*: i.e., of the newly published poet concerning the parlous voyage he as his book has audaciously embarked upon.

l.29   *flotsam on the empty page*: therefore not "empty," another paradox; also like Ishmael on Queequeg's coffin in those pages of the epilogue, empty and unwritten for the British edition till Melville in his embarrassment added "flotsam" to his wreck explaining how the story he tells survived a final catastrophic sinking into silence—else a "voluminous conceit."

ll.29–30   *words/like headstones*: the signant/cygnant headstone as the archetype of *trace*, alluding to the tomb/*tomber* of writing; also to *sema* (Greek portent, grave, gravemarker, token, seal, pictorial device) and thereby to semen and seamen (but our lips are sealed); also to the difficulty of keeping one's head above water in the wake of literary and critical discourse.

—by Jay Farness

FINALLY

With no small o to graft to its foot, the F will never be
    a sixteenth note. In this, it resembles death. There
    will be duration, but no tone.

The I, as always, stands alone—solipsistic and aloof.
    Notoriously private, even with friends, it maintains
    a singular point of view.

I envy the N its spirit of community and compromise. It
    could have been the last letter, ending things there,
    but bent over backward to be otherwise.

Such architecture rivals heaven for symmetry and grace.
    The soul will fly through the A's open eye. The body
    will crawl between its legs.

They are like two feet on a tightrope. They are like two
    crippled nails. No wonder they travel together,
    the L's; no wonder they never stand face to face.

A pair of arms that holds nothing. Lone leg on which to
    hop. Y is a question better eschewed, an embarrassment
    that should zip itself up.

4

Hide-and-go-seek

Friends forget. I am my own friend for a while:
A child reciting numbers to a tree.
Others leave. The others are not here.

I cannot find them, no matter how I stare
Into each face of every face I dream.
They hide themselves inside themselves. They disappear.

I call their names. Their names drift back to me
Like ripples on a lake before it clears.
Friends forget. It is my own voice I hear.

I cannot keep them, cannot . . . See
How they scatter like leaves in a breeze?
Reflected in a lake, the tree is bare.

Others leave. I think they must forget
The child whose recitations root him here.
He is my friend. We walk together for a while.

For a while we walk together by a lake
Where faces swirl like leaves, then disappear.
Their common voice drifts out into the night:

You left   forgot   are not here

With Shadows

This woman's face
is like a mask of a face.
I think she has composed it.

She is dressed in black
and standing on a street
in San Francisco, in 1952.

The city smells of oil and sulphur.
There is a battered taxi
idling at the curb,

its driver bored
and dreaming of a fare
that will take him south

through Bakersfield and Barstow,
then east into the desert,
into Las Vegas—

that oasis of luck,
blondes and hard silver—
then anywhere.

The woman dreams,
if she dreams at all,
of the cruise ships and steamers

that leave every day
for Osaka and Bangkok,
Madras and Shanghai;

dreams of jade and curry,
rosewood and silk,
and of a rice-paper diary—

each blank, brittle page.
It is noon and the shadows
are taking a break.

They collect beneath awnings
and the hoods of parked cars.
All morning they've reeled

themselves in from the west.
They have somewhere to go
and will get there by dark.

There is a knot
of tourists at a bus stop nearby.
They study their watches

or stare at their shoes
as though this were not San Francisco,
but a postcard of San Francisco

that could be bought by anyone
with a spare stamp
and not much news.

As though this were not 1952,
but a memory of 1952—
each detail noted

and safe from revision.
As though time,
like the shadow it is,

stood still,
and nothing could alter
the composition.

Zombies

I don't even know the name
of this plant so common
it must be second nature
to any nature poet
worth his pollen.
It has managed
a small white flower.
I keep it in the bathroom
on a rickety table
I scrounged from the dump,
where it gets next to
zero sunlight
and too much of the morning's
squint and stumble.
The last stiff to live here
left it to me,
and I have mainly ignored it
as I've mainly ignored
the bums and drunks
that haunt like novice zombies
the streets of this town.
It has endured the winter
in a room without heat.
It has survived
on ashes and grime.
It has been toppled
and uprooted twice at least.
I don't know how it
goes on living
in that shallow plot,
turning its leaves
as if they were hands,
as if they could cling
to a smidgen of light.
Those zombies must be slumped now
in the alley back of Sunshine Mission,
stretching their arms

as though to pull themselves up.
This half-dead plant
must be growing, even now,
toward the room's one window
painted shut.

Wood for the Winter

Cutting

Taking only the fallen
and standing dead,

we scavenge the forest
like scrupulous thieves:

one to buck,
two to tote—

trespassers gritty
with corporal need.

Time and again
the time-weathered wood

yields to the bite
of chainsaw or ax.

We take what we came for—
never enough—

leave without shadows,
steal our way back.

Splitting

Grained hands
to grained wood,

we heave ourselves
at the heart of things

as though the fervent
salt of work

could return the earth
its fertile seed.

The round splits clean
when the stroke is right

and the wood divides
like bread.

In exhaustion
we absolve ourselves

and woodchips
settle like rain.

Burning

To begin small
is always the trick—

match to tinder,
kindling to log—

until the knots blare
like specious eyes

caught by headlight
on a lost road.

To believe in fire
as a kind of grace

is to drift like smoke
in an empty hall,

is to enter the flame,
its quadrille of light,

through which the hand moves
feeling nothing at all.

Philly's Garden

Before I quit the neighborhood
I'll plant a flower in Philly's garden
because it's the last thing
he'd need or want and because
it will never be strong or pretty
as the flowers Philly grows.
I'll carry it in a dixie cup
one night next spring
when the moon is full for luck
and hidden for stealth.
I'll disguise myself
among the roses and the zinnias.
I'll breathe in private like the mums.
Philly will be up late
reading his Burpee's, playing his Mozart.
He won't hear me moving
like a leaf beneath his window.
He won't see me
working at his yard like a chuck.
It will be a flower I nudged
with my amateur-musician hands
from a shady spot in the woods
Philly might have walked to
when his legs were spry,
his lungs good.
It will be a flower so common and dull
you'd have to look twice
to notice it once,
you'd have to fall down
on your hands and knees
among the nettles and the burdocks
and look it in its flower-eye
to know what it is.
Philly looks like a small old man
in the garden he's tended
near seventy seasons.
He looks like the one
wizened leaf on the maple

he planted in my yard
as a sapling first,
then twice again
for each year it was hurricane-felled.
He has planted a life
in a town others visit
a month at a time, three at most,
and seldom in winter.
He planted most of the shade trees
along the east end.
To the sick and well alike
he has ministered
hollyhocks and lilacs.
He has planted for the feeble
of body or heart
the dead animal-friend.
Because he left his porch light on
nights I was out late
walking so as not to slump,
humming not to howl,
I'll poke at the earth
with my hack-horticulturist fingers
and scoop from it a shallow hole
to bed the weak thing down.
I'll stand there a minute,
maybe an hour, feeling what it's like
to be well-rooted,
green and cared for—
before I steal across the drive,
before I pack and go.
And if a flower could stand
for a man, maybe that weakling
flower could stand for me,
for Philly is a good gardener
and a good neighbor,
and it could grow
for Philly's decency.

Whatever It Is

Near the end we'll travel as two old men
Leaning lightly on one another for support—
One of us gone a little milky-eyed,
The other a little deaf.

We'll pack what we need in a cheap valise,
Taking turns so it's not too heavy.
When one of us tires, we'll stop awhile
And build a fire to warm our hands.

You'll have then to describe to me
The woods' deep green, the cobalt sky.
I'll point you where the nighthawk calls
So that you see what I hear, so we know . . .

Whatever it is we come to,
We'll travel toward together.
So when we're knocked apart at last
Something of each will go with the other.

Two old men hunched to the curve of the earth
And biding a little time between them—
Here is my shoulder steady for you,
Even this long since we started the journey.

5

Sure the Oak

is critical.
This morning, waking early
from some bad dream
I'm lucky not to remember,
I opened the curtains
to a livid dawn.
And there it was,
lopped limbs and all,
framed by a grimy windowpane,
lit by a mustard sun.
Even through smudged glass
I could see how snow
swaddled its base—
a crazyquilt of weather
broken here and there
by tree stump, bramble,
dog shit, or rock:
a cynical nativity.
But the oak
drew the eye upward—
its gnarled hide unblemished
by any green thing,
its top branches brittle
as pencil lead,
a nest there
abandoned to ramshackle leaves.
But for the oak
I'd have missed it then:
a dim fleck of motion
high overhead—
bird-like but wingless,
angelic but drab—
trailing no shadow,
bucking no wind.
Most of the morning
I watched it ascend

like visible prayer
in a deep, dreamless sky—
cold earth beneath
for the body's long sleep;
oak tree between
for the spirit to climb.

Then Again

suppose the soul is a stone
and not the holy cellophane
I've fancied it,
and thus—like the body
shorn of heat, stripped
even of the heart's
flimsy flam—
does not hover, waft, ascend,
breaststroke its way
into a panoramic hereafter
(flourish of French horns
and the multitudes joined
in a sheepish rendition
of the Twenty-third Psalm).
Yes, I think the soul
is a stone and sticks
with the body,
frazzled compadre.
And that is why we shut
the dead behind doors
without knobs
and chuck them in holes
and snub them.
That is why we leave
pages of marble
or even small houses
atop them—
to press them smooth,
to weigh them on their way.
It is the soul
steers the body,
scuttles it so
it won't be recovered
by the sharpest shovel,
the deepest sigh. . . .
And heaven is a dark place
hidden somewhere
in the earth's hard gut

where a few stones,
the lucky ones,
roll together finally
and are still.
And that is why I keep
always a few pebbles
buried in my pockets.
You could call it
honoring the dead.
I call it getting started.

Almost Dancing

In this kind of wind
blowing hard from the west—
sloughed off the Pacific
to dust the desert floor,
collecting all that chaff and grit
and whatever else a wind needs
to huff headlong into these mountains—
even the half-dead, lackluster pines
bow a bit from their stiff waists,
begin to dip and sway;
their boughs nodding together
like the heads of drunks
with nowhere to go
between last call and their dark, bolted homes—
the last bars of a two-bit tune
blowing from the jukebox—
almost touching because of the beat,
almost dancing. . . .

I was the kid with two left feet
in a school where most of my classmates
majored in meanness
and the stupefying logarithms of sex.
I held up the wall at the senior prom
while the other kids grooved
and ground their groins
like interchangeable parts
in some competent, well-lubed machine.
Even the chaperones shuffled their feet.
Even the sober, undrinkable punch
shimmied like a little sea.
The band played poorly on secondhand instruments
they'd eventually hock
for bus tickets out of town.
I would have left
if I had known where to go.
I would have danced if anyone had asked me.

How simple it looks out there
from in here: back and forth, to and fro.
Not the old-fashioned box step exactly,
but some facile choreography
starting low in the roots
and welling up through the trunk,
branches and twigs of every green
and once-green thing.
Likewise the beer cans dumped by the road
and the stop sign on its one metal leg
stir to the vagrant music of March—
the whole world a dance hall
for whatever moves with ease.
How simple it looks out there,
and yet—
what's here to move me to unlock the door,
unlock my bones some
and take the first step?

What's here to move me back
to the N.C.O. Club in Selma, Alabama—
nineteen-seventy-whatever-it-was—
where I sat with my parents
listening to the Ink Spots,
a band fallen to low-rent gigs
for homesick GI's
and blowzy town girls no one would marry?
It was the first time we got family drunk
and when the game-legged guitarist
kicked the group into "Maybe,"
that graying, corpulent couple
who'd brought me up
breezed to the center of the empty floor
and fell into each other
like falling in love—
dancing so lightly I held my breath,
afraid they'd blow away.

I'd never seen them move like that—
so many moves I've missed.
So many steps I might have learned
by stepping with my wooden feet
into the fanfare of the world,
to let its music play me green.
Maybe the wind that drums these walls,
frets the glass
and whistles down the chimney pipe
could find me with its restless riffs—
take my breath away I mean—
and lead me from myself.
A lithe wind,
a measureless wind
agog with grace notes of seed and decay,
leading nowhere
I could follow for long,
away. . . .

The Gulls

For the sound of them you'd think
the gulls know something about sadness.
All they do is cry. All they do is
rock between their spindly legs and blink

as though befuddled by their own racket.
You'd think they'd know to just shut up
and fly. Their bones are white
balsa where you find them on the beaches.

Their tracks litter the sand. They perch
on rocks like cold, bedraggled angels.
You'd think they'd know the world's no
place to land. I've stood once or twice

like a gull with my feet in the water
and my face in the wind. The salt
air stung my eyes. I've straddled the tide
and ridden it as far as it would take me.

I've cried to hear myself cry.
What the gulls lack is imagination.
Each evening when the sun goes down
they think it's for the last time.

They are unappeased by stars
toward which their wings could lift them.
They're unappeased by moonlight
in which their feathers almost shine.

Roden Crater

A day and a half we lugged those pipes—
a hundred fifty pounds apiece
of gunmetal-gray Korean steel—
lugged them, shoved them, drug them,
cussed them finally through cinder and sand,
through gaunt cholla cactus
that nibbled our ankles and up
the crusty grade of the bottom-most ridge.
Two thousand plus of them, ten foot each:
from a low-flying plane it must have looked
like some slow-motion godgame of pick-up-sticks.
Our job was to replace the waterline
that ran a mile and more from a well
up and over and into the thing,
with the desert wind whistling
for its supper of bones, and the sun
on our heads like a ton of hot bricks.
Our job was dirty, draining and dumb.
We did it for nothing, did it for art.
We knew it was art but it felt like work.
It looked and tasted and smelled like work,
like every peanut-paying, back-busting job
I ever swore I'd never do again.
What we were doing was "sculpting" a crater
in a landscape of volcanic slag
so primitive and grim we had to squat
on our heels not to blister our butts,
had to scrabble and scrounge like lizards
for enough shade to collapse in.
We collapsed. We revived. We evolved
in reverse: shedding clothes
like worn-out skin, thinking from our bowels.
We thought we understood our end,
had devoured the literature, digested the plans:
according to someone, "the Sistine Chapel
of America"; to someone else,
"the Stonehenge of the nuclear millenium."
In a hundred degrees of brain-broiling heat

the sum of *my* thoughts for the future
was getting home, a bath, some sleep.
It was hard to dream of the dead
conic mess twenty, a hundred, a thousand
years hence: a tunnel gouged
through the guts of the earth; "skyspaces"
there like picture windows onto the universe.
The universe. Damn. How to dream of that
sprawling state, its black flag unfurling
on every horizon, its anthem
of silence to deafen the dead?
How to dream fast-forward through some
twelve thousand years: the new gods, the new
extinctions, the insouciant do-si-do of the stars?
The North Star having strayed by then
and a new, perhaps more brilliant star
to steer some burned-out worker home. . . .
There'd be a place to pinpoint *that*
in a place already eons old.
Or exiting the tunnel in the bull's eye
of the crater bowl, the sun precisely aligned,
you'd swear you were walking out on the world
and into a heaven made wholly of light.
I had no experience to measure it by, but
for a movie I saw as a squirt: *The Mole People*,
a race of mutants so long underground
darkness had made blisters of their eyes;
light was lethal. Fallen into sudden holes,
our heroes blundered the length of the film
down every blind alley in that buried town
until, at long last, they're collared and sentenced:
the Tunnel of Death was a torturous
tease, a hike into the waxing dawn.
I wouldn't know art if I fell in it
but know that movie worked for me;
for all its schlock and cheap effects
it kept me wide-eyed all the night,
checking the closets and under the bed.

Imagination made me sweat.
I forged the oomph for one last climb
up and over the crater's east wall—
dragging my shadow along by the heels,
breathing double-time—
to watch the Painted Desert
burn away into the smoke of night. . . .
I might have been a Moleman then,
or at least a kid who believed in them—
that's how mortal and measly
that time-warped vista made me feel,
alone up there with nothing
to look forward to but darkness
and a long haul home, a couple winks,
then back to the university where I teach
each year more of what I understand less.
Still, there was a moment or two,
perched at the peak of that desolate place,
when I thought I understood as well
as probably I ever will
that where we live and breathe and sweat
is a blind rock lunging through space. . . .
And thought I understood, for that,
what had drug us to Roden Crater
with nothing to leave in the world but our work
and nothing to take out of it forever.

A Lick and a Prayer

in memory of James Wright

That sweet embittered man
had more poetry in his bones
than you could shake a stick at.

And you could shake a stick at
his bones, now, twisted and corroding
down beneath the dirt he sometimes loved.

I have loved sometimes
a thing or two and one
was merely human,

and offered up prayer
like so much junk mail—
how bland it grew, and snide.

The man didn't have a prayer
to speak of, yet spoke
with care. And isn't it prayer

is a kind of careful speaking,
like God was somewhere out there
with—instead of angels—stamps?

Hello. Hello? Oh, God
damn it to hell he swore
he heard a dog say once

and I believe it—who believe
more and more that less
and less is worth a lick.

And yet—you know the phrase—
we *make* believe, make do
and love if we're lucky.

This morning I got lucky.
All that rain, then light
dripping from the branches

making the whole world shimmer
and okay. Out I went walking
among the other dead

and living bones.
Sometimes you get lost in so much light.
Sometimes a stick points the way.

Notes

"A Teapot" is in memory of Alma Flowers.

"Child's Grave, Hale County, Alabama" is based on Walker Evans's 1936 photograph of the same title.

"Fetch" is in memory of Lo.

"The Swallows, Their Song," "December," and "Even the Silence" are for Becky Byrkit.

"Against Derrida" is a poetical satire of deconstructionist criticism. Jay Farness's *Glosse* of "Against Derrida" is a deconstructionist satire of the poem. Thanks, Jay.

"With Shadows" is an improvisation on Dorthea Lange's 1952 photograph "Mother and Child, San Francisco."

"Philly's Garden" is for the venerable Philly Alexander, lifelong resident of Provincetown, Massachusetts, and gardener extraordinaire.

"Roden Crater" takes as its subject the Roden Crater Project, a work-in-progress by space and light artist James Turrell. Located on the periphery of the Painted Desert in northern Arizona, Roden Crater is an inactive volcanic cone which the artist is sculpting into a natural celestial observatory. The writer has assisted in several phases of this project, including the replacement of a waterline used to landscape the crater's bowl.

"A Lick and a Prayer" takes its account of the talking dog from *A Secret Field: Selections from the Final Journals of James Wright*, edited by Anne Wright (Logbridge-Rhodes Press, 1985).

"Five Love Poems to No One," "Wood for the Winter," "Whatever It Is," "Sure the Oak," and "Then Again" grow out of a correspondence-in-verse between the writer and his friend, poet Mike Pfeifer.

Photograph by Paula Jansen

Jim Simmerman received a B.S. in Education
and an M.A. in English from the University of
Missouri and an M.F.A. in Creative Writing from
the University of Iowa Writers' Workshop. He is
the recipient of writing fellowships from the
Arizona Commission on the Arts, the Bread Loaf
Writers' Conference, the Fine Arts Work Center,
the National Endowment for the Arts, and the
Port Townsend Writers' Workshop. His first book
of poems, *Home*, was published by Dragon Gate
in 1983 and was picked by Raymond Carver as a
Pushcart Writer's Choice selection in 1984. A
chapbook of his poems, *Bad Weather*, was pub-
lished by Ocotillo Press in 1988. He lives in
Flagstaff, Arizona, where he directs and teaches
in the creative writing program at Northern
Arizona University.

OTHER GALILEO BOOKS

What Happens, poetry by Robert Long
Sandcastle Seahorses, a children's story by Nikia Clark Leopold
Life in the Middle of the Century, two novellas by John Dranow
The Halo of Desire, poetry by Mark Irwin
The Eye That Desires to Look Upward, poetry by Steven Cramer
The Four Wheel Drive Quartet, a fiction by Robert Day
New World Architecture, poetry by Matthew Graham
The Maze, poetry by Mick Fedullo
Keeping Still Mountain, poetry by John Engman
On My Being Dead and Other Stories, by L.W. Michaelson
The Intelligent Traveler's Guide to Chiribosco, a novella by Jonathan
    Penner